Eating for Better Health

By Myrl Shireman
Illustrated By Kathryn Marlin

COPYRIGHT © 2007 Mark Twain Media, Inc.

ISBN 1-58037-374-7

Printing No. D04131

Mark Twain Media, Inc., Publishers
Distributed by Carson-Dellosa Publishing Company, Inc.

Level 6: Book 5

All rights reserved. Printed in the United States of America.

Healthy Lifestyle

Eating the right foods is important if you want to live a healthy lifestyle. Those who eat a balanced diet usually look better, feel better, and have more energy than those who don't. You must choose foods that provide protein, carbohydrates, fiber, and fat. Daily exercise is also part of a healthy lifestyle.

Protein

Protein builds muscle and helps develop cell structure. A diet with the right amount of protein is very important to the normal growth of young people. However, if you eat too much protein, the excess is stored as fat. Excess fat can lead to becoming overweight. The right weight for one's height and age is part of a healthy lifestyle. To maintain the proper weight, you must eat a healthy, balanced diet. Not overeating and regular exercise are the keys to maintaining a proper weight.

When planning your diet, you should be aware that there are essential proteins and nonessential proteins. **Nonessential proteins** are made by the body. **Essential proteins** are not made by the body, so it is essential to get them through the foods you eat. How do you know what foods are sources of essential proteins? These proteins are found in foods like eggs, meat, milk, cheese, nuts, and beans. Meat is a good source of essential protein. The best meat choices for a healthy lifestyle are fish, chicken without skin, and lean meat. The size of meat portions should be about three ounces. You must take care not to eat too much protein from meat. Weight gain and higher cholesterol levels are only two of the possible problems from eating too much meat.

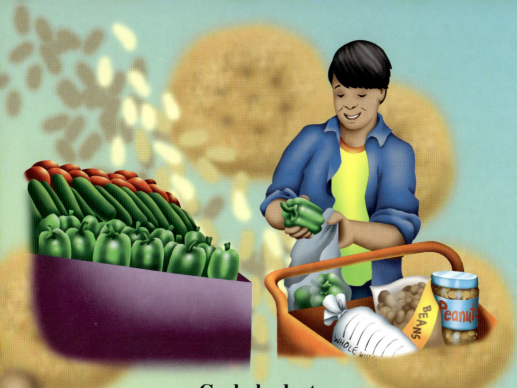

Carbohydrates

Have you ever wondered why we eat carbohydrates? **Carbohydrates** are a source of energy. They also provide vitamins, minerals, and fiber in the diet. Fruits, vegetables, and whole grains found in cereals and brown bread are carbohydrates. Bread made from whole grains may range in color from black to brown. The texture of whole grain breads is coarse. The dark color and coarse texture is because the endosperm, bran, and germ are retained as part of the bread. White bread is refined, so the bran and germ have been removed, along with many of the vitamins, fiber, and minerals. Those who make whole grain breads a part of their diet are less likely to be obese. They are less likely to have heart problems and diabetes. Whole grain crackers and whole grain foods like wild rice, brown rice, whole wheat, and whole oats are also good choices.

Fiber

Most people do not eat enough whole-grain carbohydrates. Therefore, their diet does not include enough minerals, vitamins, and fiber. Many fruits, vegetables, nuts, beans, and whole grains contain **fiber**. Although fiber should be part of a healthy diet, fiber has no food value. Fiber is important because it adds bulk to your diet. Fiber is more filling, making it less likely you will eat more than you need. Fiber also aids in the passage of food through the intestines. A diet that includes fiber may help prevent diseases such as colon cancer, diabetes, and heart problems.

How do you get more fiber in your diet? Think about eating more fruits and vegetables. When you increase the amount of fiber in your diet, you may at first experience some discomfort. However, this discomfort passes quickly as your body gets used to the new diet.

Fats

Fat is also a source of energy and is a vital part of a healthy lifestyle diet. However, eating too much fat can lead to weight gain. Excess weight may lead to diseases of the heart, diabetes, and some types of cancer. Did you know fats may be saturated or unsaturated? For example, **saturated fats** are found in animal meats and dairy products. These fats are solid at room temperature. A diet that includes too much saturated fat increases the risk of heart trouble and stroke. **Unsaturated fats** remain liquid at room temperature. Unsaturated fat is found in olive oil, canola oil, sunflower seeds, soybeans, and peanuts.

The amount of fat in the diet must include a balance between saturated fats, monounsaturated fats, and polyunsaturated fats. A diet for a healthy lifestyle may include fat from all three of these fat sources.

The amount of saturated fat in the diet should be limited to ten percent of the daily fat intake. An increase in fat from monounsaturated and polyunsaturated fat sources, like olive oil, canola oil, sunflower seeds, soybeans, and peanuts, is encouraged. Fat is part of a healthy lifestyle diet. However, the amount of calories from all types of fat should be limited to one-third of the daily diet.

Many fish contain omega-3 fat. This fat is good for the heart. A healthy lifestyle diet should include fish on a weekly basis. Herring, cod, and salmon are fish high in omega-3 fat. However, you should avoid eating certain kinds of fish that contain high levels of mercury.

When food is processed, the fat in the food goes through a change. The change may result in **hydrogenated fats**. These fats increase the cholesterol level. When buying foods, read the food label. It will tell you the amount of hydrogenated fat in the food item. These fats are most often found in foods like margarines and shortening. Foods with hydrogenated fat should be limited in the diet.

Sugar

You may be thinking about the sugar in your diet. Too much sugar in the diet is one of the main causes of obesity. Sugar in the diet increases the number of calories. However, sugar has little food value. Candy, soft drinks, jams, and jellies are often very high in sugar. Any processed food may also be high in sugar. Excess sugar results in an increased intake of calories with little food value. This leads to weight gain. A healthy lifestyle diet limits the amount of sugar.

Weight Loss

If weight loss is your goal, then you must reduce the calories eaten. You must still eat a healthy diet, but you must select foods without high amounts of sugar and fat. Eating low-fat foods may also help lower cholesterol and avoid heart problems. Eating a proper diet is the first step toward weight control and better health.

Starving yourself to lose weight is not part of a healthy lifestyle. A healthy diet includes a balance of protein, carbohydrates, fiber, and fat. However, you can gain weight while eating a healthy diet. Therefore, to reduce weight, you must eat a healthy diet and not eat more calories than needed on a daily basis.

Salt

Americans have always eaten large amounts of salt in their diet. In earlier times, salt was used to preserve meat and to keep it from spoiling. As a result, people developed a taste for salt. Most foods today contain more than enough salt, yet the salt shaker is found on most tables. A healthy lifestyle limits the amount of salt in the diet. Too much salt often leads to high blood pressure, which is a major cause of heart problems and stroke.

A key to limiting the amount of salt in the diet is to become a better grocery shopper. Many cheeses, packaged meats, and soups contain large amounts of salt. You can check the labels of packaged or canned items to find the salt content. A diet for a healthy lifestyle should not include more than 2,400 mg of salt each day.

Recommended Servings

Everyone should try to include more fruits, vegetables, and whole grains in their diets. The amount of sugar and salt should be limited. One of the main causes of being overweight is eating more than is needed. The United States Department of Agriculture (USDA) and the Department of Health and Human Services (HHS) list the following as recommended serving sizes.

BREADS, RICE, CEREALS, AND PASTA
<u>1 serving</u>: 1 slice of bread; 1 ounce of ready-to-eat cereal; 1/2 cup of cooked cereal, pasta, or rice

VEGETABLES
<u>1 serving</u>: 1 cup of raw leafy vegetables; 1/2 cup of cooked vegetables; 3/4 cup of vegetable juice

FRUITS
<u>1 serving</u>: 1 medium apple, banana, or orange; 1/2 cup of chopped, cooked, or canned fruit; 3/4 cup of fruit juice

PROTEIN
<u>1 serving</u>: 2 to 3 ounces of cooked lean meat or poultry; 1/2 cup of cooked dry beans; 1 egg; 1/3 cup of nuts

The Food Pyramid Guide below, created by the USDA and HHS, is a guide for the number of daily servings from each of the food groups.

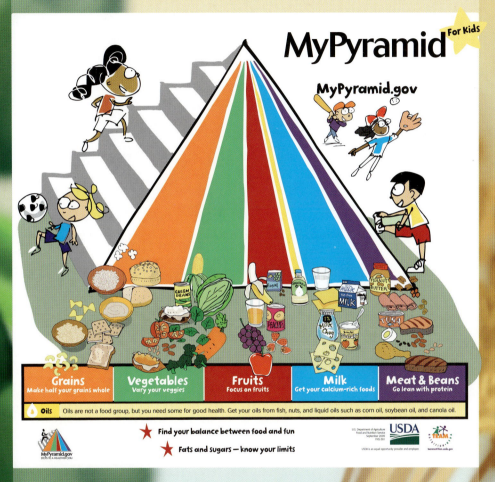

High cholesterol levels and high blood pressure levels make heart problems and strokes more likely. A healthy lifestyle diet can improve cholesterol levels and reduce blood pressure. A healthy lifestyle helps you control weight, feel better, and have more energy.

Blood Pressure

When the heart beats, blood is pushed through the arteries. Blood is also moving through the arteries between heartbeats when the heart is at rest. If the arteries are blocked, then the heart must pump harder to push the blood through the arteries. A blood pressure reading gives two numbers, such as 120/80. The top number, called the **systolic pressure**, is the blood pressure when the heart is beating. The bottom number, called the **diastolic pressure**, is the blood pressure when the heart is at rest between beats. The higher the blood pressure numbers, the more difficult it is for blood to move through the arteries. This causes the heart to work harder. High blood pressure is a primary cause of heart problems and strokes. People of all ages should monitor blood pressure levels. Blood pressure may vary from time to time. It is best to take a number of readings and find the average. This will give you a more accurate blood pressure reading.

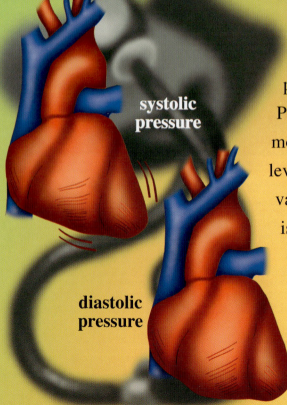

systolic pressure

diastolic pressure

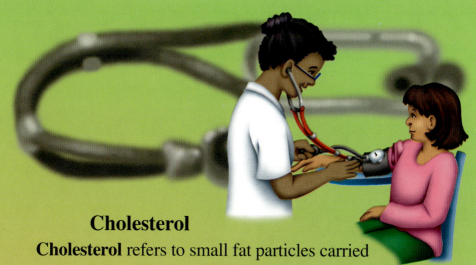

Cholesterol

Cholesterol refers to small fat particles carried in the bloodstream. The small fat particles are known as **lipoproteins** and **triglycerides**. Triglycerides are the fat found in most foods and in the body. Any calories eaten that are not used for energy are changed to triglycerides and stored as fat in the body. If you eat more fat than you use, you will have high triglycerides. A blood test shows your triglycerides.

Cholesterol levels are also checked using a blood test. The test gives a reading for total cholesterol, but the test should also give a reading for both LDL (low-density lipoprotein) cholesterol and HDL (high-density lipoprotein) cholesterol. A high LDL reading means that fatty deposits may be building up on the artery walls. This will restrict blood flow and could lead to a heart attack or stroke. For this reason, LDL is often called the "bad cholesterol." HDL is often called the "good cholesterol." Fat is carried by the HDL to the liver, where it does no harm. A healthy lifestyle helps lower the LDL level and increase the HDL level.

Total Cholesterol: below 200

LDL cholesterol: below 100

HDL cholesterol: above 60

Triglycerides: below 150

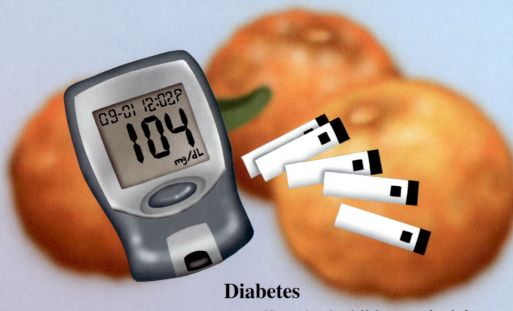

Diabetes

Diabetes is a disease that affects both children and adults. Today, many young people are overweight. A healthy diet is not part of their daily lives. As a result, Type 2 diabetes has become more common among young people. Type 2 diabetes occurs when the muscles, liver, and fat do not use insulin properly. When this happens, the amount of **glucose**, or sugar, in the blood increases. The test for diabetes is a blood test that checks the level of glucose in the blood. A high level of glucose may indicate a diabetic condition. The symptoms of a possible diabetic condition include frequent thirst, weight loss, tiredness, and the slow healing of cuts and bruises.

You have learned that to live a healthy lifestyle, you need to eat a balanced diet. By following a healthy diet, you can prevent high blood pressure, heart disease, and diabetes.